CHEER THE F*CK UP

FRESH OUT OF FUCKS

Keep that shit up!

The fucking sun will come out tomorrow

FUCK WHAT THEY THINK

BE AWESOME ★ AND ★ GIVE NO FUCKS

Fuck it, let's color!

SMILE, ASSHOLE!

CHEER THE F*CK UP

Positive Sh*t to Color Yourself Happy

A SWEAR WORD COLORING BOOK

ST. MARTIN'S GRIFFIN
NEW YORK

www.stmartins.com

ISBN 978-1-250-14173-6 (trade paperback)

Our books may be purchased in bulk for promotional, educational, or
business use. Please contact your local bookseller or the
Macmillan Corporate and Premium Sales Department at
1-800-221-7945, extension 5442, or by
e-mail at MacmillanSpecialMarkets@macmillan.com.

First Edition: February 2017

20 19 18 17 16 15

KEEP CALM AND
CARRY THE FUCK ON

SHIT HAPPENS

Tomorrow's a new day to be your best damn self

GET THE
HELL OUT
OF YOUR
OWN WAY

YOU ARE A
BOSS BITCH

Live the shit out of life

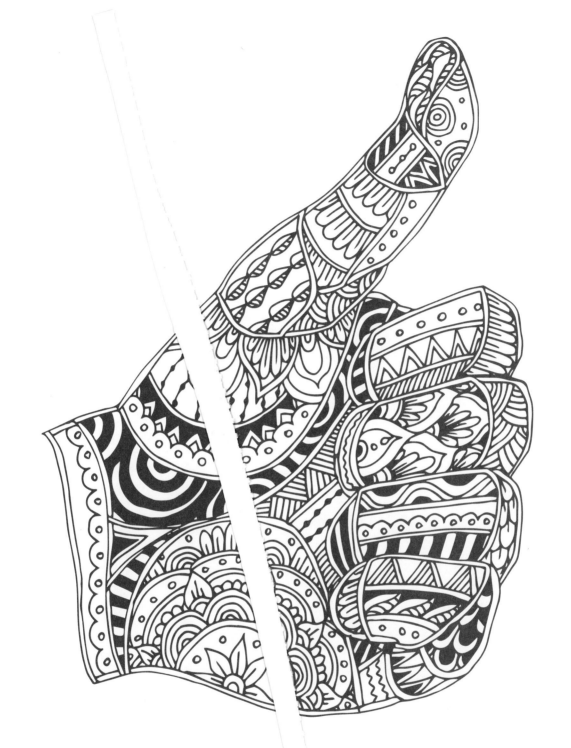

IT'S GOING TO BE A
GREAT FUCKING DAY!

YOU ARE A BADASS

When life hands you lemons,
squeeze those bitches into your vodka

YOU MAY FEEL LIKE SHIT, BUT YOU LOOK FUCKING FANTASTIC

The fucking sun will
come out tomorrow

YOU'RE BEAUTIFUL, BITCHES!

*Where did I leave
my goddamn tiara?*

It's called a breakup
because it's fucking broken

NOBODY DOES IT
FUCKING BETTER
THAN YOU

KEEP THAT SHIT UP!

Be awesome
and give no fucks

Don't let
the bastards
grind you
down

GO THROUGH SHIT, GROW THROUGH SHIT

AFTER MONDAY AND TUESDAY, EVEN THE CALENDAR SAYS WTF

FUCK IT, LET'S COLOR!

FUCK WHAT
THEY THINK

Drink up, buttercup

Bitches get shit done

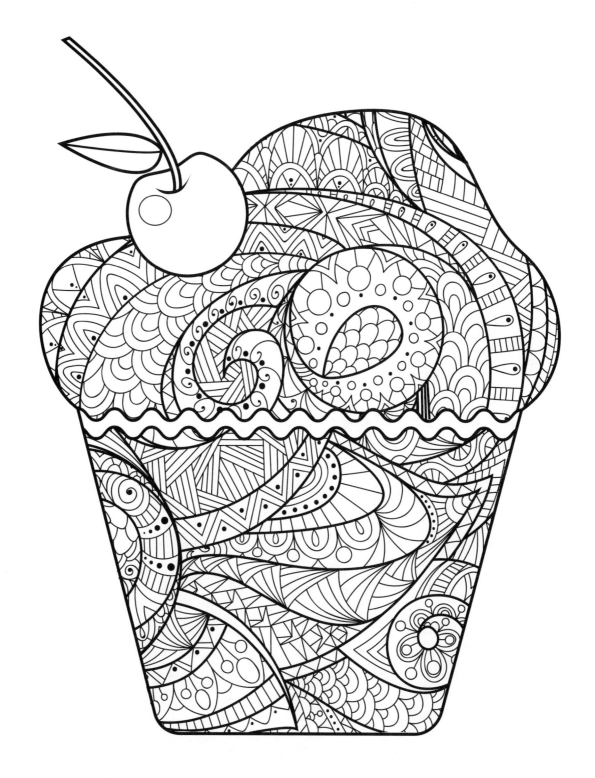

You're someone's
reason to masturbate

YOU PROBABLY NEED THESE, TOO

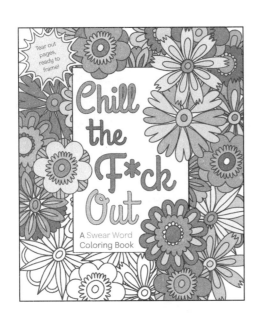

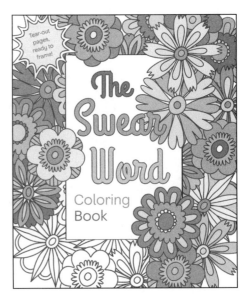